Elliott Carter

Figment III

for Solo Contrabass

HENDON MUSIC

AN IMAGEM COMPANY

DISTRIBUTED BY

HAL•LEONARD®
CORPORATION
7777 W. BLUEMOUND RD. P.O. BOX 13819 MILWAUKEE, WI 53213

www.boosey.com
www.halleonard.com

for Don Palma

FIGMENT III

for Contrabass

Elliott Carter
(2007)

Rev. 18 July 2007

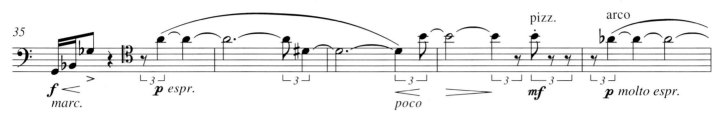

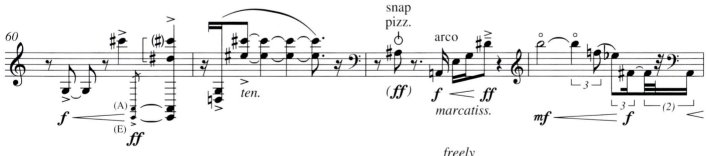

CARTER: *Figment III*